My Blue Sweetie

poems by

NEAL ZIRN

Finishing Line Press
Georgetown, Kentucky

My Blue Sweetie

Copyright © 2024 by NEAL ZIRN
ISBN 000-0-00000-000-0 First Edition
All rights reserved under International and Pan-American Copyright Conventions. No part of this book may be reproduced in any manner whatsoever without written permission from the publisher, except in the case of brief quotations embodied in critical articles and reviews.

Publisher: Leah Huete de Maines
Editor: Christen Kincaid
Cover Art: Neal Zirn
Author Photo: Neal Zirn
Cover Design: Elizabeth Maines McCleavy

Order online: www.finishinglinepress.com
also available on amazon.com

Author inquiries and mail orders:
Finishing Line Press
PO Box 1626
Georgetown, Kentucky 40324
USA

Contents

Sleeping Together 1
Tom Cat Blues 2
Decisions 3
Reunion 4
Dark Places 5
Tableau 6
Your Indigo Kiss 7
Our Space was our Prison 8
Soft as Silence 9
Hearts with Wings 10
Kiss Me 11
Germaphobe 12
Drinking the Moon 13
Runner 14
Love Lost 15
It Had Become her Thing 16
On Your Leaving 17
Secrets 18
Beets 19
Insomnia 20
7 A.M. 21
Tattoos on His Calves 22
Preparing to Move 23
Down and Out Latte 24
The Ghost of Relationships Past 25
If Looks Could Kill 26
She took the lonely 27
Cubist Delights 28

Four Years Max	30
My Blue Sweetie	31
Frame It	33
At a Thai Restaurant	34
Blue, Like Little Boy or Baby	35
Like a Bird	36
It Was Like That	37
Last Song	38
Shot in the Back	39
At the Supermarket Checkout	40
Sunday Mornings	41
Your Long Piano Fingers	42
Blue Balloon	43
Remembering a Long-Ago Girlfriend	44
Fetish	45
Your Lollipop Man	46
Hotel	47
The Park	48
If We Loved Each Other	49
Your Eyes	50
On Going to Russia to Adopt a Child	51
Woman in a Café	52
Dinner at the Blue Moon Diner	53
On the Winter Solstice	54
Blonde, Like Doris Day	55
Lost Meeting	56
Wedding Invitation	57
Coffee and a Scone at the Angry Eggplant Café	58
Woman with Red Hair and Freckles	60

For all the women who have forgiven my trespasses

Sleeping Together

The evening, already late, is
a dark oyster in a half-shell
of palm leaves, wrapping itself
about us like a blanket of pearls.
The wind raps against the window
causing it to quiver. Your legs
are like copper snakes, smooth
and winding around mine.
Your breath is like an accordion,
and your hair is twisted in my hand,
tight, until you sigh for our lives,
our musk dreams and our flowers
made of sand. We are drifting,
on a bed of feather sheets in a house
with tin floors and walls as tall
as the black cliffs of midnight.

Tom Cat Blues

I know you liked the timbre
in Tom Waits voice, soaked in the spirit,
like Louie Armstrong, and blouses that
showed off your shoulders—the type
you only see in old movies on women
with mega-earrings and long flowing
skirts who know how to tango and rumba.
And that you also went for what you labeled
Sensitive New Age Guys and believed I still
had too much Bronx left to deal with, which caused
me to wonder about your affection for old Tom Cat.
And all those many evenings you spent wandering
up and down Bourbon Street and Kentucky Avenue
looking, for what you thought was, the heart of Saturday night.

Decisions

"Do you want to spank me,"
she asked, pulling down her pants
and lifting her ass towards the ceiling.
We had argued and this, I thought,
may have been her way of making up
to me.

We had played some games before,
but her suggestion was something
new and exciting. I didn't know
for sure if she was serious, mocking me,
or pushing the envelope in front of my face.

When she wiggled her behind and said,
"Honey, you have to decide what you
want to do," I was at a loss for words.

Some things go without saying.

Reunion

You were surrounded by hummingbirds;
a natural woman in that small town,
high in the mountains, with its quaint
shops and restaurants, lined up along
the main street as if they had nowhere
else to go, gray-streaked clouds rolling
by above us.

You kept snapping pictures, attempting
to capture the day as if it were a fugitive
on the run; eating impressions; your mouth
smeared by the sun and the beating of wings.

It was a strange reunion, lovers, now distant,
from another era when we were newly minted
and shiny, graceful and without memory,

free from where we were now: in a fathomless
portal we never knew existed.

Dark Places

I liked living in dark places,
cellars were fine, bunkers
were even better.

It was good to hunker down
and become the shadow
I always wanted to be,
like a fly on the wall
or a passing vision
without any details.

Being unknown was something
I valued, having the ability
to come and go undetected
and take what I wanted,
without any consequences,
fit my idea of how life
ought to be.

When I robbed you of your innocence,
you never really noticed.

It made you happy,
although you didn't know why.

Tableau

If you looked hard enough,
you could see the stillness
as if that which is hidden
had become manifest,
as if quiet, like a stone statue,
was right there beside you.

There was no time to waste,
because there was no time;
like rose petals in a windstorm,
blown away into that which we
are unable to describe, fluttering
like the wings of a hummingbird
as it traces the sign for infinity.

And you, remaining in that element,
part of a tableau, a motionless dancer,
a ballerina in black tights and a wry
smile, searching for an audience.

Down on yourself, hoping to find me
in the cool of the evening.

Your Indigo Kiss

Your indigo kiss,
cool in the light
of a blood moon
rising, your patchouli
love, like a breeze
on a sea of sunflower
blossoms surrounded
by cliffs of turtle shells
and lapis lazuli, is soft
like a drop of awareness
on my forehead, as I
close my eyes to the bright
truth of springtime and fathom
the looming chasm between us.

Our Space was our Prison

You were the hotel: the lobby,
the bar, our room that looked out
at the nunnery across the street.

It was all done with intention.
The excuses we told our spouses,
and the secrets that we kept
from each other.

Our space was our prison,
confining us within a circle
that kept us from being
what we had become.

Like two pieces of a broken cup,
we tried to fit, despite the lack
of anything that could hold us together.

We wanted.

What we got was more
than we deserved.

Soft as Silence

You wore your wings
as if you wanted
to fly away, and never
have to feel the loss
of light, or the darkness
of betrayal.

Of course, they were part
of the illusion that you carried
on your back, like a parachute,
ready to open at the first sign
of things not going right, for you.

There were also the bells,
attached to your toes,
that jingled as if every day
were Christmas, announcing
your presence, reminding me
that you were a force to be
reckoned with.

When you disappeared into the clouds,
like the morning star, you became part
of the mist, then fell to Earth along with
the rain, soft as silence, like the flesh
in the palm of your hand.

Hearts with Wings

There's the sad, and the empty,
and hearts with wings traversing
the skyways as if love were a blessing
to be had by all.

Being serene, and still as a tall oak
on a windless landscape, I can sense
the motion inherent in the atom,
the new moon rising from a dream,
and the one life in many,
and the many lives in one.

When I have that transcendental feeling
that you are standing, like a totem,
outside my door, your auburn hair
cascading around your shoulders
as if enlivened by an unknown force,
I know you are there; fourth chakra open,
blue on a shifting and ever mutating background,
a lonesome spirit hanging out in the grim part
of town.

Kiss Me

She would be the last one.
I told her that after an upset
followed by a two-hour conversation.

She said that I had ruined her
for other men, as if there could
have been others after me,
but now not so.

We said we were the loves
of each other's life, that had
we met when we were younger
we would have married and had
children; two being the right number.

Je t'aime, she would whisper
in my ear. We liked to communicate
with the little bit of French we knew
between us.

"Kiss me," she often requested
at times; unscripted and in the moment.

And yes, sometimes she said in the throes
of passion that she would do whatever I wanted,
whatever struck my fancy.

It was like there was more than one cherry
on top of the sundae. Too much, but not enough
when it really mattered.

Germaphobe

She had that germaphobe thing,
hand sanitizer before meals,
using her shirttails to turn a doorknob.

It was as if her environment were
a cauldron of disease, bubbling over
with that which infects.

A trip to the hospital was something
that sooner or later was going to be inevitable,
sirens blaring, dodging traffic like it was the draft
in times of war and pestilence.

But she did have a face that reminded me
of a Modigliani painting, and legs as long
as my imagination would take me;

sometimes down Relationship Alley,
sometimes leading towards a world
of sterilized codependency.

Drinking the Moon

You drank the moon from a silver cup,
and it went down easy, like Jack neat.

And it heightened the feline qualities
you already possessed, your intuition
and your aloofness, your ability to land
on your feet no matter how high you were
thrown into the air.

In some ways, it enhanced your attractiveness,
and in some ways, it seemed to create an edge
that could cut into whatever you desired,

to damage your prey at will, then capture him
for your amusement, bring him to your lair,
and own him like he was always there for the taking.

Runner

She knew how to run; gracefully, elegantly,
and exquisitely, with long strides,
and a swiftness that was part of her nature,
deer-like and naturally free.

It was as if the wind were always at her back,
and she could create distance out of the very thinnest
of air.

It was a task for the foolhardy to attempt to catch up
with her, such was her ability to get away from that which
she deemed threatening, disturbing, unnecessary,
or requiring any sort of commitment regarding her resources.

Infatuated, I once thought I knew her, but perhaps it was only
the smoke and mirrors she left in her wake.

Like the phases of the moon, she reflected the light back to me,
a light I was not prepared for, but that nevertheless existed.

And when she ran, silently and barefoot through the woods,
under cover of dark, unknown, even to herself, it was then
that I felt the closest to her, as if she were the night,
and I had become her shadow.

Love Lost

Love lost on the Great Mandala,
turning like a roll on a pianola.

Maybe it was the intensity of the relationship,
a firebird rising on wings of polished steel,
that caused the fall from grace, and the recognizable
uncertainty.

When there is nothing left to hide,
and nothing left to say, a door opens
to a vastness that sees without eyes
and hears without ears.

So, if I ever meet you again, I believe
it will be in a place where retrograde
is the rule, and all things reverse themselves,
to come to rest where heaven and earth,
thunder and lightning, began as a point
in the mind of God.

It Had Become Her Thing,

sitting on the stoop in front of her house
just before sunset, letting the twilight wash
over her as if she were a stone at the bottom
of a waterfall, while waiting for him to appear
in his black SUV, the one she remembered him
driving in the now distant past.

Perhaps, you might think that what she was doing
was a bit pathetic, watching for a man who had left
her, but I like to imagine her devotion as being akin
to the Amish custom of putting out a place setting
at each meal, three times a day, for a family member
who had left the fold, even if it had been many years
since the person in question had last been seen.

It was, then, a matter of faith, a golden promise she
had made to herself that all was not lost, and that
it was good and proper to keep a light burning
in the window as a beacon for him when he sought
to return,

and as a comfort for him when nothing else would suffice.

On Your Leaving

Things end. Except for those that don't.
Like the serpent's circle or parallel lines
that never meet.

It is said that the Buddha experienced
a hundred-thousand past lives the night
before he attained enlightenment, and that
we exist within an infinite past that is behind
us and an infinite future that is in front of us.

You may believe that something is over,
but truly, that may not be the case. I ask,
what can eventually cease that never really
began?

Your leaving was like the autumn leaves
that have fallen to the ground, and have been
covered up by the first snows of winter,

waiting for the thaw to be revealed.

Secrets

Walking in the foothills,
together, you wearing that wide-brimmed,
floppy hat, which cost you dearly when you
flirted with what amounted to a salesboy,
right in front of me, as if I were your cuckold,
and you were my hotwife, even though we
were never married.

Step by step, stride for stride,
we negotiate the path, with wild grasses
marking our way, grey clouds overhead
like boats without sails, drifting: the day
a circle, your tenseness palpable,

the wind blowing by us like someone we
can't remember, like you with your secrets,
and your thinking about things you think
I don't know.

Beets

I told her over lunch
at our favorite restaurant
that I hate beets, the same way
that I hate the cold, as well as coleslaw,
rap music, and licorice.

And we both agreed
that we weren't very fond
of cocoanut

It was as if I had confessed
all my sins, and deep as the center
of the Earth secrets to her, and that
she was finally getting to know
who I really am.

Except that I left out the part
about how I loved her turned legs
in her cut off shorts,
and her gray-brown hair
that circled her shoulders
and ran down her arms
just above the elbows.

But that's a story for another day
and another time.

Isn't it?

Insomnia

She'd taken half a sleeping pill,
and still, she couldn't fall asleep.
Her thoughts were like lizards,
slithery, prickly lizards, that crept
across the outskirts of her mind
and nestled into crevices wherever
they could find one. He had left
three weeks ago saying he had
had enough, of *what* she wondered,
as she turned the words over gentle
and easy, like flipping an egg
while trying not to break the yolk.
The ceiling above her creaked
and the noise from the street was
filled with teenagers raising Cain,
and the sound of a siren in a hurry
taking someone to the hospital.
She cleared her throat and felt
as if the night were sitting, heavy,
on her chest. Her feet were cold,
and her eyes were dry and gritty.
There was nothing to do but lie
on her back and reflect on their time
together, while watching the clock
change numbers in the dark as if
keeping score of something big,
and about to pay a visit.

7 A.M.

She asked, "Pancakes?"
I replied, "Fuckwheat?
Sounds good. With blueberries?"

She was a great cook and could
make anything. And knew how to
boil in the bedroom, as well. Not
like the last one who was bad
in the kitchen and worse in the sack.
Like lying down with nothing special.
It hurt sometimes.

We sat around the kitchen table
and laughed about my choice of words.
And what to have for breakfast.
Her hair was curly vermillion,
and her front teeth gapped,
which was strangely attractive to me.
She said she loved me like a m.f.
and that she knew I liked to chat up
the women, but that that was OK with her;
I didn't know what I was doing.
Her two big labs, one black and one chocolate,
bookended me as I drank my coffee.
The sun hit my back through the sliding glass
door, as if it knew, exactly, where I was.

And she did too, for a while after that.

Tattoos on His Calves

Her son was a wrestler, sporting orange-red hair and tattoos
on his calves. A Jewish mother, with Jewish guilt, Jewish
anxiety, and all the worries from the Patriarchs down
to the present. She told me that she went to some of her
son's matches, but we never got to go to one. Issues, break-ups,
reconciliations, and a final ending to a hammer-hold relationship,
preventing me from ever seeing her son wrestle. Perhaps,
all for the best.

She'd tell her friends and relatives that her son had graduated
college, which he said he did, although she wasn't really sure.
And avoided, if she were able, the topic of wrestling. Still,
people were curious, as it was somewhat of an oddity; a Jewish
lad breaking chairs over opponent's heads.

And a mother with a lock on something, she couldn't quite
put her finger on.

Preparing to Move

She was all *this and that,*
fussing along like a ruffled hen,
wrapping heirlooms in tissue paper shrouds
then placing them in cardboard boxes,
the past a blood-eyed fox seated on a crooked log.

Mother's china and glassware, a couple of menorahs,
all the wines and liquors that mother left behind,
were among the items to be "taken with."
Sandwiched in were figurines and photo-albums.

I watched and helped her seal the boxes with packaging
tape from her hand-held dispenser. Each box was marked
as to content and room destination. It felt like *karma on the go,*
earlier sins and sorrows, family and otherwise, ready for
re-assignment.

Regarding her, it was business as usual. I don't believe she realized
what she was moving; her entire world contained in all those
little boxes, then stacked to death in her spare bedroom.

The sun shining in through open blinds.

Down and Out Latte

You went into your sad café,
the one you like to call *home,*
and ordered a rueful croissant
and a down and out latte
with a shot of angst.

Memories of lost loves
and all the times you thought
you'd been done wrong
sat down with you at your table
and sang, in harmony, that old
familiar song about lonely nights
and don't want to get up mornings.

Flustered, you dropped your croissant
on the floor and spilled your latte
on the table.

A sorry for yourself feeling
took hold of you like a bulldog
with a bone and wouldn't let go.

Sighing out loud, you wondered
if things could get any worse.

Although, a part of you thought
your situation was just the way
it ought to be, just what you
so desperately needed.

The Ghost of Relationships Past

I woke up in the middle of the night
with a woman, big as a basketful
of schizophrenic monkeys, sitting
at the foot of my bed, beckoning
for me to come hither.

She was only there for a brief moment,
but she reminded me of the few women
I have known who set their sights on me
and had me in their crosshairs, waiting
to pull the trigger.

It was as if the Ghost of Relationships Past
had paid me a visit, just to inform me
that some things never go away.

Like promises made that have never been kept,
or love's illusions that continue long after
their expiration dates.

I cringed and pulled the covers back over my head.

Sometimes it's best to let sleeping dogs lie
in order to keep them from barking,
and biting you where it's going to hurt the most.

If Looks Could Kill

You were sitting in my lap,
blonde and petite, people sneaking
glances at us, as we waited for a table
in the restaurant, when you answered
a call from your pre-teen daughter,
telling you to come right home,
that your mother had died
from an aortic aneurysm,
quick and relatively painless.

At the hospital, you viewed the body,
collected her belongings and got on
with things—calling siblings, friends,
other relatives, and fussing about
with whatever needed to be done.

After the funeral, you kept putting off
seeing me, saying mirrors reflected badly
on you, and that I wouldn't want to be with you
the way you were, which wasn't true,
but which was a belief you adopted
as if looks could kill, or something like that,
which they did, as far as the relationship went;

a bad hair day and a lack of makeup,
as deadly as a stray bullet from a thirty-eight special.

She took the lonely

pill and got a house
with many rooms
and a gas station
across the road
where Friday night
kids screeched their tires
and next door
they could buy coke
from mustachioed Greeks,
or so she said.

Her cigarettes smoked and
cubes rattled in tumblers
while cars with horns
and sirens blasted vociferously
(no malaise that year)
but by winter there
wasn't much sun
and the street became
dark and quiet early.

That was when I
liked to stay upstairs
and listen to the night
black against the window.

Cubist Delights

Martha appeared to me
last night in a dream,
boyish hair, banged
but not broken, impish,
petite, and good as ever.

We sat at a small table
by a window without
a view, set to dine
on cubist delights.

Her kids, whom I never
met, were somewhere
in the house and her ex
was there as well.
I didn't have a shirt on,
so, Martha got one from
her ex's closet, a blue
short sleeve which
I refused to wear.

We sat across from
each other, smiling like
our teeth would break,
indifferent to her kids,
her ex, and the house
that surrounded us.

Were we in Toronto?
Or upstate New York?
Or were we in the future
in a place that never existed?
I asked Martha, but she didn't
know, so I grabbed a handful
of faceted cherries, took a bite
from a blue squared fish,
and washed it down
with ju-ju juice.

And it all tasted good.
So very, very good.

Four Years Max

The women have come and gone
as if they were on a punch clock
that only allowed them to stay
for a preordained period of time.

Usually, a year was the minimum
and four years max. My behavior
didn't seem to be a factor regarding
how long the relationship would last.

I mean, bringing flowers, listening
to their complaints until I felt that my aura
needed disinfecting, participating in public
displays of affection, avowing my adoration
on a regular basis, and performing to my utmost
when it came to sexual liaisons, didn't amount
to squat, a hill of beans, or whatever else could be
put in the pot, as to the cohesiveness of the union.

Things would often fall apart as if a malevolent force
had descended from the skies and tore at the bonds
of our togetherness. This would frequently occur
after an intense, amorous weekend and would leave
me reeling like a man on a carousel gone haywire.

No, the gods kept crushing the little enjoyment
I derived from being with a woman, as if the fix
was in from the get-go.

Karma? Maybe.
Me? Also maybe.

Or just plain bad luck at the roulette wheel
of romance, in the gambling house of love.

My Blue Sweetie

She was blue,
blue hair, blue skin,
blue eyes, blue heart,
blue, blue, blue.
Cerulean, ultramarine,
sky blue, cobalt blue,
blue as a woman could be.
Blue in b-flat, yes,
that's how she was
and that's the way
I knew her.

She would put on
her blue lipstick,
blue nail polish,
and her blue dress
and we would go
downtown like that
to see a sad movie
and have a coffee
in a sad café.
I was miserable
anytime I was with her
and wore this misery
as my own blue overcoat.
And oh, to feel so bad
it was almost good,
that's how I knew
I was truly alive
and suffering
as I should be.
Lord have mercy
on my soul.

And then one day
she was gone
as if one season
had ended and another
was about to begin.

She said I was
too unhappy for her
and that she needed
to be with someone
who made her laugh.

Well, maybe the next
one will be green
or yellow.
Although red
would be nice,
rosy and all that,
you know.

Frame It

The beginning looked like raspberries
and ice cream. Doesn't it always.

Everything was long; your hair,
your legs, your fingers, the nights
we spent in each other's arms.

The foothills seemed to have a voice,
the wind whistled, "Come hither."
The sun rose and set, and it was good.
The moon had her night, and hid her secrets
behind her many phases.

Children skipped rope and repeated
nursery rhymes, keeping a rhythm
as we sat side by side
in restaurants and jitterbugged
to rock and roll in the kitchen.

Death didn't seem as heavy,
and every person, place, and thing
took on a life of its own.

The world vibrated,
and sang a song of Now.

Time was.

And came.

And went.

And we both,
in harmony,
disappeared into the rolling clouds
as if nothing ever happened.

At a Thai Restaurant

The snow was coming down, "Blue roses
and funny valentines," I thought, "my life."
She held me by the arm, the wind swirling
the snow around forming circles that disappeared
then re-formed, only to disappear once more
like galaxies being created, destroyed, and
re-created again.

She continued to keep her hand in the crook
of my arm as we climbed the stairs to the restaurant
and, finally, were in out of the cold. I hadn't seen
her for almost half a decade and here we were,
lovers for an evening, seated at a table, her hands
covering my outstretched hands as if she wanted
to hide them from the public and make sure she had
them all to herself,

the room glowing softly, the traffic in the street
visible from our elevated view, every woman
I have loved in my time, standing, it felt,
as reminders of reunions past, behind me,
while I gently withdrew my hands, looked over
the menu, and waited, like a man who has always
been in too much of a hurry, for the waiter to arrive
and take our order.

Blue, Like Little Boy or Baby

I couldn't afford the three years,
spent as if I had fifty more, a few
good stories, and that was it. Weekends.
Things never went beyond being together on weekends,
you, me, and menopause caused insomnia.
A bad dream and a brutal laugh.
The condo, the Metro, the theatre, the restaurants
and cafes, dancing down Cote Saint-Luc Boulevard
without any trousers. Your skirt between your legs,
pinching at your thighs. The beginning, the assertion,
more than weekends, lost, like a blue note from an
existential horn. A sad tune played on a broken sidewalk.
Nothing in the bank but an old, copper penny. Friends
from the far side of abandoned relationships. Eggs and prayer
for breakfast, a side of OCD, and a cup of woe. Toil and
Trouble waiting in the hallway. Susie and Boozie and Minnie
and Molly, all your gal pals from way back when. Members
of the Men Are Wicked In Their Ways Club. Shopping
and mopping, and all that razzmatazz. A Montreal moon,
and in bed by nine,

these days.

Like a Bird

She has a nervous laugh,
and laughs at points
in the conversation
that are devoid of humor.
She always wants to appear
agreeable, one of the little
people, but she has a position
that is high above most of them,
reminding me of a bird sitting on
the uppermost ledge of a skyscraper,
a bird with a golden beak, dark
plumage tinged with grey, breasts
that suggest inverted teacups, and
very long legs, quite pale, but long.

I want to believe that her nervous
laugh concerns me, that she feels it
in her solar plexus as if a nest of snakes
had been let loose to slither around
inside, that she senses the trap I've set
for her that would tear off her wings
and feed them to the dogs, and that if
she ever came close; I'd lock her in her
fear, toss away the key, and put her
in a cage, where she would sing for me
like a tone-deaf diva in a three-penny opera.

It Was Like That

It was like that in those days,
living on Horatio Street in the Village,
gentrification a few decades away,
everything *cool* before *cool* was something
anybody knew about.

Things were popping on the streets,
MacDougal and Bleecker,
and The Fat Black Pussycat was,
well, The Fat Black Pussycat.

You were from the Upper West Side,
folks with a summer place in Kennebunkport,
looking a bit like a young Kate Hepburn,
hanging out with the commoners,
digging on me as if I were a bodhisattva
in a turtleneck and bellbottoms.

Which suited me just fine, a woman
who knew how to take care of her appearance,
soft on the outside, a little naughty on the inside.

Staying at your parent's penthouse on West End Avenue
when they were out of town, watching at night as the lights
were put to bed on the Empire State Building,
thinking of you with the shades down and all your secrets
exposed,

as if you believed you never had any.

Last Song

We'd sing "You Are My Sunshine" together,
dance cheek to cheek or jitterbug in the kitchen
like kids in high school, and sit in a booth
side by side when we went out to eat.

On the surface, it was all happy, happy; no blues
or sad country songs, nothing but open skies
and angels beneath our wings.

My friend Len told me once that if you're rolling
in a bed of roses, watch out for the thorns.
"Hell is other people," as Sartre liked to say.
I should have known,

when it comes to women with issues,
you might as well sign me up. Does it have
something to do with mother? Am I living
on cloud nine without knowingly owning a parachute?

And, now that we are communicating (at least I am),
if I ever see you again, I will pretend that you are Lady Yin
and I am Dr. Yang, and that I do, indeed, make house calls,
and that everything fits together perfectly, just as we always thought it
would.

Shot in the Back

You got out your relationship gun,
the one that separates the boys from the girls,
and with not quite Annie Oakley precision,
shot yourself in the foot and me in the back.

There was a lot of confusion as I went down,
our friends and relatives gathering around me,
wondering what happened. I could sense them
all staring at me, thinking I must have done something
to deserve my fate, their eyes wide open like they
were about to see the Ghost of Relationships Past
enter and possess me, body and soul.

As I gasped for air, I could see some of your friends
tending to your foot, and heard them consoling you
with the idea that you did the right thing;
blood on the ground, no blame to speak of.

At the Supermarket Checkout

She's been chatting with me on the supermarket
checkout line when she tells me how she sometimes
runs out of money by the end of the month because
of vet fees, and food for her cats and one lonesome
male dog.

I ask her how many cats she has, and she answers,
"Forty." She's a schoolteacher; fair of face, nice
to look at, with a smile that has me smiling
right back at her.

I'm new to Denver, and it would be a joy to meet
a woman I could spend some time with; dinner, a movie,
a pleasant walk in the park. In the past I seemed to have
attracted women with issues, as if I went by the name
Sigmund, and had a pocketful of answers.

I was hoping a different locale might change things.

There's a café in the supermarket, and before she mentioned
the cats, I was thinking of asking the teacher if she would like
to have a coffee with me. But now I'm not sure, and wondering
about that solitary dog, and what, in the name of sanity,
he's doing in that house.

Sunday Mornings

The kitchen would bustle on those Sunday mornings
when I had stayed overnight, the bed sheets tossed carelessly
about as if they were props that had already fulfilled their purpose.

If there was a breeze blowing in from the foothills, the aspen trees,
that graced her front yard, would flutter coquettishly until the leaves
began to emit a whistling sound, apparently without a care,
like newly minted young sailors embarking on their first extended
shore leave.

A large, multi-colored Buddha sat by the corner window and filtered
the morning sunlight, casting rays of happiness upon the floor
tiles, creating a sense of possibility.

She liked to monitor the eggs frying upright in a pan, and flip them carefully,
making certain they were served over easy, while I prepared the toast;
buttered or with jam.

Shortly after breakfast, as was my choice, I would leave for my home,
a gourmet chocolate bar in hand, a going away token for the coming weekend
and all the time we would spend apart, unaware of the distance, gathering
space, between us.

Your Long Piano Fingers

You had those long piano fingers,
slender and delicate, although you never played.
Your legs, too, were well shaped, as if turned
by a master on a lathe made for creation.

That was when I first met you, but pressure
and circumstances, like a two-headed cobra,
turned you into a wisp-like shadow,
lengthened by the sun and cast upon the ground,
thrown down haphazardly as your piano fingers
extended themselves, reaching for the things
they believed they could not have.

As you continued to age, the fingers became gnarly
and the legs shaky. Your hair took on streaks of gray,
and your mind became suspicious. Strange motifs
began to play in your head, and visions of those who came
before appeared at intervals then faded to black.

When you thought you heard a distant sonata, you engaged
by humming along, while your fingers ran across a wooden tabletop
as if it were an ivory keyboard.

Blue Balloon

Somehow you were able
to place yourself inside
a blue balloon, float miles
above the skyline, and look
down on the, now, little
people; the crowd that once
possessed you, homogenous,
with cruel intentions, gasping
for air, twisting, as if wrung out
of rope, on the sidewalk.

It was like you were jacked up
on helium, your voice surreal
and squeaky, your consciousness
like a carousel, turning around
in time to hear the calliope music
you believed to be playing for your
ears only.

I had tried to grab the string,
attached to the balloon as you
began your ascent but was unable.

It all happened so quickly;
the spacing, the timing,
the last chance to get hold
of you.

Remembering a Long-Ago Girlfriend

Twenty-five years ago, we bought a house together,
a home on a corner lot. You purchased a Yorkie,
that almost died, for five-hundred dollars from a puppy
mill pet store. Hard earned money later spent on vet fees.

You didn't leave me much closet space, maybe because
I was only there on weekends, still working out of town
in order to make a living. The basement had been finished
and had a bar that we never used, although you liked your beer
and cigarettes when you came home from your job.

You said you lost yourself a long time ago, which meant little
to me at first, but turned out to be a red flag that foreshadowed
that the relationship would eventually unravel.

And it did.

And it's true, that after that I never saw or heard from you again,
and that I don't think of you very often now that the tide, so to speak,
has gone out to sea.

Except for today, when a quite distinct picture of you, your blonde hair
in a page boy, ran through my mind as if you were in a hurry
to get to the next lifetime.

As if you had decided it was important, and wished to see me
one last time.

Fetish

I guess you could call it a fetish,
we all have them, even if we consider
them as distant relatives who never
leave the house; agoraphobic entities
that crawl around inside our heads.

For him, it was women in pleated skirts,
knee socks, and penny loafers. He thought,
perhaps, it was a reminder of the Catholic
school girls he rode home with on the Number
One bus that made its way along the Grand
Concourse to Mosholu Parkway, down Sedgwick
Avenue, and came to a stop at 231st and Broadway.

But, maybe, that was too simple a theory.
The knee socks etc. were one of the standard
outfits the women in college wore, back in the day,
and it was the flesh between the top of the socks
and the skirt that attracted his fancy, and the place,
naturally, he wanted to touch.

Recently, being much older, he dated a woman
who needed compression socks that reminded him
of knee socks. They joked about it, and she teased
him as to how they satisfied some of his desires.

She didn't mind wearing them to bed, and was quite
generous in that respect.

You could call it love, but that might be stretching
things a bit.

Your Lollipop Man

I think I'll keep it short, or not,
I don't know yet. It seems I write
about you more often than is healthy,
especially those long legs of yours
that never stop going, and never stop
running away from that *thing* we thought
we had.

I was sort of like your lollipop man,
if you know what I mean; sweetness
on a stick, not necessarily necessary
to sustain you, a treat in the middle
of an uneventful day, something
you wanted but were reluctant
to admit to.

Some of your friends said they hardly
recognized you since we'd been together,
had never seen you laughing and smiling
so much. It appeared as if an invisible being
tickled you at the oddest moments; under
your arms, the soles of your feet, the parts
of you that rarely saw the light of day.

It was quite the opposite of the photo
on your driver's license—a dour face
that gave the impression you had been
possessed by The Ghost Of Everything
That Ever Did You Wrong; your past
lives and past loves, crawling over
your skin like some predatory force
with a thousand toes, and a head as big
as an all-day sucker.

Hotel

The hotel was fine.
It had once housed railroad workers,
but had experienced a makeover
and was now chichi, pie a la mode fancy,
coffee and croissants for breakfast.

We had a suite of rooms
that overlooked a park with a bandstand
and a rushing river that came down
from the mountains, and was often used
for rafting by folks looking for excitement
and adventure.

The bed was a king,
and we made good use of it.
Being older, we took our time
and knew how to stretch things out,
making sure we touched all the spots
that needed to be touched, including
the wounds that never want to heal.

You seemed at home
in a strange place, taking in the view,
giving the impression that we had always
lived here, that somehow this is how we
spent our existence, as if we were permanent
residents in an unknown country where
everything constantly remained the same.

And where the bandstand was forever
filled with music, playing long into the night,
and an invisible circle surrounded the town,
making it impossible for us to leave, so that,
over time, we came to understand
that there was no way out of our situation.

The Park

We stayed in a suite
of rooms, overlooking
a park with a bandstand,
in this small town
with a river running
through it like a thread
from halcyon days
and gypsy nights.

We watched as children
passed their afternoons
laughing and shouting,
unaware of their futures,
free in a way that we would
never be.

When the evenings arrived,
a crowd would gather
and dance in circles
as a group played on,
and with a frenetic energy
that caused the windows
to rattle in our hotel bedroom.

By the time the park emptied,
and the moon had risen,
as if it knew how much
we longed for it to arrive,
our affection for each other
had increased in intensity
and incorporated our feelings
from the pleasures of the day,

the children, the dancers,
the park and the dream
we call summer, the waxing
of the light, and the lengthening
of the shadows.

If We Loved Each Other

You had those long legs,
long arms, and long hair,
long fingers too, that I thought
of as piano fingers, even though
you didn't play.

It always seemed like we were
in that honeymoon phase
that people talk about,
when we weren't what we had been,
as if we possessed new minds
and new bodies, wings on our feet
that took us away, surrounded by
a mysterious ring that kept us
contained within ourselves.

The light that endures,
pierced our surface
and briefly gave us hope.

If we loved each other,
it was, like most loves,
a strange love that had
its own life, its own ways,
its own time, and its own
cross to mount and live with.

It enabled you to shine
even more, stretch your fingers
as far as they would go,
and reach for us,
and the darkness hidden inside
our shadows.

Your Eyes

There are the photos of you on Facebook,
thin strands of gray hair partially covering
your head, and another one of you, taken
on the same day, which looks like you're wearing
a wig made of curls—my first thoughts being
chemo? Perhaps. And your weight—at least thirty
more pounds added since last I saw you. Wide
waisted, and seemingly caught in the headlights
in an old lady's dress with a bland, floral pattern.

A long way, indeed, from the bar at the Seafarer's
Hotel, 1984 or thereabouts, nursing your gin and tonic,
cranberry red top, shoulders revealed as if the secret
of our affair was about to go public; black pleated skirt,
matching pumps, legs crossed at the ankles, waiting for me
like I was the only man who ever was or would be,

with your mars black hair framing your face as if sketched
in charcoal, lips conveniently parted, and that *something
about you-here I am* quality encircling me like the dancers
in a Matisse painting.

That weekend spent hardly leaving our room; takeout Chinese,
bed unmade, protected for a time from death and taxes, dark love
and lust atomized into the air and permeating our existence
like a living organism we could never get rid of, the optimism
of connection being what we had going for us.

And today, seeing that you're married and quite different
from the woman I once knew; rolling on, which is something
to be reckoned with, your eyes, still vivid and clear,
looking far beyond the physicality of now.

On Going to Russia to Adopt a Child

I said I'd go with her to the Mohawk Smoke Shop
to buy cigarettes, Marlboro being the brand of choice.
Cartons of them. They were cheaper on the Rez.

"You need them to bribe the officials with,"
she said. "That's what they told me at the agency.
And I also have to bring 10,000 dollars in United
States currency. I bought a money belt to wear under
my blouse so I can hide all that cash when I go."

Besides buying the cigarettes, she picked up
some trinkets to use as gifts. When we got back
to my place, I carefully stacked the cartons
of smokes on the kitchen table. They reminded
me of boxed ammunition, ready to be used
whenever necessary.

"Still sure you don't want to go with me?"
she said. "I'll pay."

Even though I'm part Italian, it was another
offer that was easy to refuse. "Have to work, babe.
Can't afford to take time off. You know that.
We've talked about it."

'I know, but well, I'd really like you to come along."

Outside some jerk was screeching his tires,
and in some other world, that I imagined as being
next door, we were definitely having a different
conversation. She was a single woman who wanted
to be a mother, so much so, that she said, "Waiting
to adopt a child was almost like being pregnant."

I sat down for a minute, closed my eyes,
and considered my reply. If I wasn't careful,
pretty soon she'd be sitting on my lap and calling me *daddy*.

Woman in a Café

A woman sat in a café
near my apartment building
with nothing to do but sip a cup
of coffee, cross and uncross her legs,
and look as if she were waiting for
someone to sit down beside her.
A stranger, perhaps, might appear;
a man with her face in his wallet
that she thought she knew but had
never met. Or a person from the past
who just now flitted across her mind
like some rare hummingbird with wings
of fine, polished steel; the windows of the
café open to the street and an afternoon
breeze that entered as if a guest from a land
far away and beyond the sea.

The woman looked up briefly as she felt
the warm air embrace her skin and sensed
that she had forgotten something that mattered,
something that she could not recall. People
at the other tables were lost in conversation,
or in dining and didn't seem to notice her.
For a moment she had the strange feeling
that she may not really be there; that she
may not really exist. Then a man, seated
with another woman, glanced and then smiled
at her from the far side of the room. The smile
seemed to pass right through her as if she were
made of a transparent material, and fix itself,
she imagined, to the wall just above her left
shoulder. It then appeared to be watching her
as she finished her coffee. The man who had
lost his smile, turned his head toward his
companion and continued with his meal. The
woman, after staring at the man and the smile,
again, got up and left, leaving a generous tip
as well as a napkin with an impression of her
lips, behind, on the table.

Dinner at the Blue Moon Diner

"Fish baby, I'm going to have the fish,
grilled salmon," I said. "What about you?"

She was just the kind of woman who liked
to take her time and do things quite slowly,
including selecting her choice for dinner.

"I'm thinking about the salad," she said,
with her head cocked to one side, her index
finger alongside her cheek, and her thumb
under her chin. "Hmmm, maybe it's not that
filling," she continued. "I'm starved. Perhaps
the lasagna? Good, but fattening. Chicken?
Wonder if I can get it without the skin? Steak?
Shrimp? Hot turkey sandwich? I better leave
some room for dessert."

I didn't drink anymore, but a glass of cold beer
was becoming a possibility. "Baby, the server
has come back three times for your order. She's
starting to look like she wants to kill us with
the daggers in her eyes."

"Another few minutes, sweetheart," she said.
"I've almost made up my mind."

A woman at the next table, seated with her husband
or boyfriend, whom she appeared to have in tow
as if she were the captain of a tugboat, kept jabbing
at her salad while glancing over at our table. I felt like
it was only a matter of time before the entire diner would be
staring us out the door.

"I'm ready, honey," she finally said. "You know, we're so much
alike. Order me the grilled salmon, will you, just the way you're
going to have it. Now, wasn't that easy?"

On the Winter Solstice

From my window, I can see the crows
roosting in the tree across from me,
barren and rigid, the flow of life
having ebbed, winter rolling in.

It's almost Christmas, sleigh bells ringing
and all that jazz, everyone a salesman
(or a saleswoman) this time of year,
retail needing to make its numbers,
screw you when the credit card debt
arrives, like Vinnie and Anthony
wearing black leather jackets,
driving a Lincoln Town Car,
and informing you it's time to collect,
pal.

And, for the record, it's been just about
three years to the day when, over the phone,
you told me that our relationship was over,
and that it wasn't me, but you, Lord, have mercy
like that made a difference.

And now, again for the record, I'm lying
on my couch in my cozy apartment,
surrounded by statues of Shiva, Ganesh, Buddha,
and Krishna, all my old friends from days long past,
thinking of you during this holiday season,
with the spirit of goodwill floating in the air
like a stick of incense, burning, wishing you
a way out of that which troubles, on this
the longest, and, even though a full moon
is about to appear, darkest and most dangerous
night of the year.

Blonde, Like Doris Day

I could continue talking about her for hours but what's the use?
When you've flipped you've flipped. Like a table with a short
leg; shit shakes on it. You can put a folded-up napkin under
the leg but it never seems to hold. Shimming it with a slip
of wood doesn't work either. Once the creation isn't quite
right, you can't make it right no matter how hard you wish
for it. I know. I tried.

She liked to do things very fast or not at all, preferably
with a low-tar cigarette in her mouth and a Coors in her
tiny right hand. Zip Zip. Whip up some eggs, make the bed,
run to the store, and fold together the goddamn socks, which
was something she was forever in the process of doing.
Whatever I did, however, seemed to be flawed. If I mowed
the lawn, I left a spot. If I washed the dishes, I left a spot.
If I cleaned the bathtub, hey, you get the picture. There was
no way to please the woman even if you turned into Harrison
Ford for an evening, fucked her every which way but loose,
bought her an ice-cream sundae, and signed on to pay her
alimony for the rest of her life even though you weren't
married to her. No, baby, there was no way to win this game.

Well, she did eventually lose it and attack one of her brothers
over who got what antique after mother died, and where mom's
ashes would be spread if they were going to be spread anywhere
at all. Maybe with dad, over the Rockies, or maybe in the
driveway so you wouldn't slip on the ice. With those people,
who the fuck knows what they're going to do. But I will tell you
this, she had one hell of a smile, and she could make me laugh,
which isn't an easy thing to do. And, yeah, she was a blonde,
like Doris Day, and I hadn't been with too many blondes,
let alone one that liked me.

Lost Meeting

"I never thought I would see you again,"
he said. It was an overcast day, gray clouds
hanging about like unwanted children, the café
half-full, the barista occupied steaming lattes
and espressos.

It had been over four years, no contact, unknown
to both where the other's life had taken them,
broken pieces of *what once was* scattered
in the wind like dirty love letters written on
the leaves of the sins of omission.

She had messaged him on his cell phone,
asked if they could meet, didn't say why,
and now he was sitting across from her,
not sure what would happen, and where
they would go from here.

He glanced around the room, the lighting,
hanging from the ceiling by black, insulated
chords, shimmering in what appeared to be
an unnatural glow, the woman he thought
he once knew, moving her lips, recapping
their relationship, saying she didn't know
the reason, but somehow, she felt she
just had to see him; her time passing quickly
as part of her life drifted away, like a familiar
song she'd heard before, but couldn't quite recall
when.

They talked some more, maybe for another hour
or so, then got up to leave. It was already dusk,
and that transitional period, similar to the pause
between inhalation and exhalation, set the mood,
as they parted in different directions, still unsure
if there had been a purpose to their meeting,
the traffic picking up speed, the night,
and all it brings with it, crashing down the avenue
like that sucker punch you never saw coming.

Wedding Invitation

"How'd you like to come with me
to Baltimore? My cousin's getting
married. We'd be staying in a nice
hotel, and I'm sure we can have
a real sexy time together."

I had just met her through a mutual
friend, hadn't even been out on a date
with her, and here she was inviting me
to a wedding with benefits.

"It all sounds good," I said, "but I already
have a plane ticket, for the same weekend,
to visit an old pal of mine in Seattle whom
I haven't seen in years."

"Maybe you can go another time, another
weekend. I know you won't regret coming
to Baltimore," she said, her *come hither* voice
almost burning up the phone line.

I recalled that she was pretty attractive: nice face,
a together figure, brown hair cut in a bob. And, from what
I remember of our initial meeting; she didn't seem that
unstable to me, a budding expert on dysfunctional women.

"Let me think about it and I'll get back to you," I said,
then hung up the phone after exchanging a few more
pleasantries.

Too good to be true? Even if it was, what did I have to lose
except what usually gets me in trouble in the first place?

The obvious.

Coffee and a Scone at the Angry Eggplant Café

A tidal wave of political ads keep flooding
my TV screen as I try to watch the news
or a ballgame, the garbage so thick,
I'm drowning in it, like a man in need
of a reliably sure, patently perfect, and totally
shitproof, life preserver.

Getting off the couch, and putting on my shoes,
I decide that enough is enough, and head out
the door, determined to walk and get some sun.

Doing my typical route, going up to the college,
stopping at the bookstore for a look around,
and winding up at the Angry Eggplant Café,
I have my usual coffee with half and half,
a blueberry scone that melts, well, wherever
you want it to melt, check out the fiftyish
professor type a few tables over, sitting
with her legs crossed, who appears like
she hasn't had any in quite some time,
and begin to mull over the conversation
I had yesterday with the woman at the bank
who notarizes whatever I need notarized.

This woman at the bank had proceeded,
in an off-hand manner, to tell me a story
about her niece's son, three weeks old,
who died while having surgery to repair
a hole in his heart, and how her niece,
instead of being angry with God, which
I, as sure as hell, would have been, felt
blessed that she was able to hold him once,
for a brief period of time, nurse him,
and watch him smile his great big smile.
It almost had me turning soft, but I didn't.

Continuing with my coffee, I glance again
at the woman I believe may need something
I have to offer, who has now uncrossed her legs,
and is dangling her shoe in my direction,

think about how I'd like to blow up my TV
set with all the politicians stuck inside of it,
and, picturing that poor little boy, who wasn't
long in this world, finish my scone, tip my cap
to the simply seductive lady, and her shoe,
then ask the server for the check, and something
cool to wash this whole scenario, which seems
as if it's about to end without me getting the girl,
or indigestion, down.

Woman with Red Hair and Freckles

I can still picture you coming to visit me,
when I was living in an attic, in Portland, Oregon
over fifty years ago. I had a good view of Mt. Hood
that welcomed me every morning as if I were the only
one who knew of its existence.

You had hitchhiked all the way from Brooklyn.
You could do that back then, although there was
still the possibility of vanishing like a coin in the hand
of a magician, never to be heard from again.

What I remember most is the sun shining in through
the Venetian blinds and casting long, dark shadows
on your skin as you lay on the bed, quiet and still,
after we made love, your red hair seemingly ablaze,
and your freckles spread over your face like so many
points of emphasis.

Naturally, the relationship was never going to last
given our restless, wandering spirits that roamed
from place to place like characters in search of the end
of time, and the beginning of tomorrow.

After you were gone, I heard from an acquaintance
that you had another boyfriend for a while, left him,
had been raped by three guys on a stained mattress
in an old garage, and returned home, beaten down,
your innocence lost, like a precious locket torn away
from its chain.

And now, that is a few years ago, I read on the website
of the long defunct Screaming Zebra macrobiotic restaurant,
where I had worked as a dishwasher and you used to hang out,
that you had passed away, a victim of breast cancer, and that you had taught
at a Waldorf school. No mention of marriage, children, or anything else.

And since you had slipped my mind as if on freshly greased wheels,
for lo these many years, I had hoped for some reaction, some feeling
of loss or sadness, but there wasn't any.

All that I had, was the image of you, your face, your freckles, your beautiful
red hair, smiling at me in that attic room, as sun and shadow ran over your body
in wave after wave of contrasting rhythms, and wistful longings. Playing on
   my thoughts,
seeing us bound together through lifetime after lifetime

.

Acknowledgments

The listed poems first appeared in the following publications:

Remembering a Long-Ago Girlfriend—*Concho River Review*
Insomnia—*Concho River Review*
On Going to Russia to Adopt a Child—*Paterson Literary Review*
Your Eyes—*Paterson Literary Review*
Last Song—*Mudfish*
Cubist Delights—*The Main Street Rag*
Tom Cat Blues—*The Main Street Rag*
Shot in the Back—*Blue Unicorn*
Tattoos on his Calves—*Poetica*
Preparing to Move—*Tribeca Poetry Review*
Sleeping Together—*Ship of Fools*
Blonde, Like Doris Day—*freefall*
Blue, Like Little Boy or Baby—*Jones Av.*
My Blue Sweetie—*Barbaric Yawp*
Blue Balloon—*Uppagus*
Secrets—*The Big Windows Review*
On Your Leaving—*The Big Windows Review*

On Going to Russia to Adopt a Child and Your Eyes won Honorable Mention awards in the Allen Ginsburg Poetry Contest.

Neal Zirn was born and raised in the Bronx. He is a retired chiropractor. His work has appeared in a host of journals including *Blueline, Mudfish, Concho River Review, The Dalhousie Review, California Quarterly, Barbaric Yawp, The Big Windows Review, Sufi Journal The Main Street Rag, The Paterson Literary Review, Coal City Review, New York Quarterly* and *North Dakota Quarterly*. He has placed eight times in the Allen Ginsberg Poetry contest and been nominated for a Pushcart Prize and a Best of the Net 2023 award. His chapbook, *Manhattan Cream*, was published by MuscleHead Press. *Up North*, a chapbook, was published by Finishing Line Press.

Neal Zirn has exhibited as a painter, printmaker, and illustrator. He received a Liquitex Excellence in Art, Student Grant and placed first, and second in WCNY Art Invitationals. His drawings have appeared in *Nerve Cowboy*, and he has done illustrated chapbook covers for poets Steve Henn and William Michaelian, and poet/flash fiction author Francine Witte.

www.ingramcontent.com/pod-product-compliance
Lightning Source LLC
Chambersburg PA
CBHW020341170426
43200CB00006B/465